BRITAIN IN OLD PHOTOGRAPHS

CHEADLE

JOHN HUDSON

SUTTON PUBLISHING LIMITED

Sutton Publishing Limited
Phoenix Mill · Thrupp · Stroud
Gloucestershire · GL5 2BU

First published 1996

Cover photographs: front: Cheadle Green in
Edwardian times; back: railway workmen.

British Library Cataloguing in Publication Data
A catalogue record for this book is available from the
British Library.

ISBN 0-7509-0641-3

Typeset in 10/12 Perpetua.
Typesetting and origination by
Sutton Publishing Limited.
Printed in Great Britain by
Ebenezer Baylis, Worcester.

CONTENTS

INTRODUCTION

When you ask old people what has changed the world most in their lifetime, you will usually be answered in one of two ways. Some will talk of the growth of motor traffic, while others will tell of the wonders of 'the electric'. And the truth is that in most communities, the latter group is usually the one in the majority.

For those of us who enjoy looking at photographs and postcards from the past, with their country lanes and village streets in which children can stand and stare at the camera without a care in the world, it is hard to believe that it was not the internal combustion engine that had the greater impact. Yet when you think about it, the provision of power to every house was a far more wide-reaching, democratic process, giving even the poorest in our communities the right to a source of lighting and heating previously enjoyed only by those with the means to generate their own.

Ninety years ago in Cheadle you could count almost on your fingers the number of people you knew who owned cars, and the thought of you yourself having one – or even riding in one – was as outlandish as any dreams we might have of flitting around in a private jet plane in a few years' time. One day, maybe, who knows. . . .

As for those Edwardian views of almost empty streets, it was not until half a century on, in the 1950s, that most families of only slightly above-average means could begin to think of a car of their own, by which time electricity had for generations been their main source of any number of services in the home, the entertainment that eased their lives being by no means the least among them.

In short, the accepted wisdom is that old photographs beguile us into believing that the growth of visible motor transport has had the greatest effect on our communities of today, tempting us to overlook the civilizing power of electricity. In Britain at large I am sure that that theory holds good, but there are some parts of the country in which it is open to doubt, and I believe that the Cheadle area is one of them. How busy and bustling it is, not just in the streets and lanes that were here a hundred years ago but also in the scores of other thoroughfares that have sprung up as a direct result of the internal combustion engine. Whole new shopping areas, too, that would be nothing without the transport to bring them within the reach of tens of thousands of potential customers. What would our forefathers have made of them?

Victorian Cheadle villagers would certainly have foreseen a flourishing future for the community. As the old Queen's reign progressed, it became clear that the village was destined to be more than a mere country backwater. But who in the oldest pictures in this book would have predicted the scene in today's Cheadle High Street on an ordinary working day of the week – say Tuesday morning at eleven o'clock – with the cars, the juggernauts, perhaps even the occasional bus? Would they not have shuddered and found it too intolerable to contemplate? And when they looked up to the skies for relief and saw great birds of steel swooping down towards earth, surely they would have thought that the end of the world was nigh.

There is a picture in this book of nineteenth-century bellringers at St Mary's Church that strikes me above all others as a scrap of testimony from another age and another life. Looking into the faces of those men, old and not so old, it is hard for me to imagine any significant conversation with them. Presumably we would overcome the problems of speech forms and dialect before too long, but the chasm between our respective worlds would surely be too great to bridge with ease. With gentle prompting, our Victorian forefathers would doubtless be able to grasp the organic growth within their community from their time through the inter-war years and perhaps into the 1950s – but our age of microchip and microwave, motorways and shopping malls and street lighting that turns night into day, what would they make of that?

Would they even see it as an improvement in the quality of life? Most of us would not wish to return to their basic ways, but is it not easy to imagine that they, in turn, might shun ours with a shudder? On reflection, Cheadle in the 1920s would probably have been the ideal half-way house for them, and perhaps for some of us, too. A tootle into the village on the bike to do the shopping, leaving Maud the maid to dust around. Ah, there's Alf Perry sweeping the path beside the Rectory wall, and Mr Pollock getting out of his big old Morris. 'Morning, Rector!' Oh well, we can dream. . . .

Not that the North Cheshire of late Victorian times would have been rural in the way the term would have been understood in North Yorkshire, Devon or Dorset. Of course Cheadle and Cheadle Heath were small islands in a sea of farmland, orchards, gardens and smallholdings, but already the local economy relied on the big houses – the halls of Abney, Moseley, Stanley, Adswood, Gatley and the like – and as the railway web spread there was more work to be had from the country-loving Manchester industrialists who found a home here – work in service, or in delivering them milk, eggs, vegetables, meat, cheese, and a hundred and one other necessities for their homes, horses and grounds.

At the same time the great Cottonopolis to the north saw in Cheadle and its neighbours a healthful retreat on its doorstep in which to site its convalescent hospitals, its orphan homes, its schools and sanatoriums. Again there was a call for domestic help, for provisions, for helpers and handymen. Until well into this century you could hire a live-in domestic maid in Cheadle for 10*s* a week or £26 a year, and it was not until those times passed that the clear distinction between the local cottager families and the incomers in their red-brick villas began to break down. Today, it seems that the only way in which tradition is upheld lies in the fact that Cheadle has long been a magnet for families wishing to better their lifestyle, and that is the way it remains.

In thanking all who have helped with this book, I hope none will be offended if I make special mention of Dr George Chivers and Mrs Dora Steele, who with their differing approaches will leave future residents of Cheadle with a far more graphic account of the community's past than would have been the case if they had not made their knowledge so freely available to others. Local history is not a commodity to be locked away, and if this collection proves to be the first of several, so much the better. Cheadle is one of those deceptive places where history is never far beneath the surface – in street names, on old family shop fronts or disguised behind modern façades. There are many more faces from the past hiding out there, and may this book turn the key to their return to the community.

John Hudson
1996

AROUND THE VILLAGE

Cheadle Green in Edwardian times, with railway carriages crossing the bridge. Though much of the countryside around the village was sparsely populated, the scene here is recognizably suburban, with tram lines to the foreground and an army of bollards staked out around the green. Truly rural village greens of this time were simply patches of grass merging into dusty cart tracks. The garage on the right displays a large Automobile Association sign of the type used by the organization until recent times.

A similar view to the one facing, with a backdrop of the half-timbered Manor House and the London and North Western Railway's Cheadle station. Wares as diverse as pianos and coffee are advertised on the hoardings under the bridge. Not for the last time in this book, the foreground has been hijacked by a group of little boys, this time with a bicycle far too large for any of them to ride. The taller young person in the smock to the left has had the left arm amputated, and was perhaps a patient from Barnes Convalescent Hospital.

The Manor House in late Victorian times, with its roof thatched, in a picture first published in Fletcher Moss's history of Cheadle of 1894. Moss wrote that some 'old men say the old timber-built house near the station was the Bulkeley Hall, and that it was always called the Manor House in their youth. As no Lord of Cheadle Bulkeley had lived in Cheadle from the time of the Civil War to 1875 . . . it is possible that the steward of the manor may have lived at this house.'

The Manor House in the earliest years of this century. According to Fletcher Moss, the railway company had reroofed it with red tiles instead of thatch, leaving the house 'improved and restored' in a way of which he seemingly did not approve. It looks much like this still today.

Cheadle Green and Fountain in the 1890s, in a view looking down the High Street. On the left, the George and Dragon is going through one of its understated phases, for at times over the years the old coaching house has looked as flamboyantly half-timbered as any building in the village.

Cheadle Fountain, put up in memory of the Victorian village GP Dr Ockleston in 1910 (see p. 97). Children would drink from the top, horses from the troughs and dogs from the lower bowls, and that was the way it stayed until well into the post-war years. The fountain was removed in 1968 to the Queens Gardens old people's flats, where it remains an attractive sight filled with plants.

The Fountain being put to good use, and the George and Dragon in one of its more striking black-and-white phases. Signs around its archway advertise both good stabling and a garage, for at this stage in Cheadle's history the horseless carriage had still not conquered the world.

The Green in the late 1950s. The internal combustion engine was clearly king by now, yet traffic does not dominate the scene in the way it all too often does today.

A scene midway along the High Street, around where the Boots store stands today. The building was occupied by a private school for boarders and day pupils, known in the village as the Red Cap School because of the boys' uniform. Lifelong resident Dora Steele, née Perry, recalls her council worker father felling the tall beech tree in the 1930s.

The High Street in the 1950s, and what familiar names for residents whose memories go back forty years or more: Seymour Mead, Needham's fruit shop, the Arcade, Heald's and John Williams' grocery on the corner of Massie Street, Alcock's outfitters then as now. . . . As for that great swathe of road to the centre of the picture, why does it seem so much more cramped and congested to us these days?

John Donald's saddler's shop in Cheadle High Street, on the site now occupied by Iceland. Horse blankets and harnesses surround his door, and his window is crammed with all the paraphernalia that helped keep horses busy on the road and in the fields. Children would peep in on Donald at work on their way home from school, and he would toss off-cuts of leather at them if he did not want to be disturbed. His sister, who lived to be 104, lived in the cottage next door.

Cheadle High Street in 1908, again showing the Red Cap School on the Boots site of today, and the beech tree close by. The house in front of the tree became the District Bank, and later the National Westminster. Trams ran along the street on the route between Stockport and the Horse and Farrier at Gatley until 1932, when the last one completed the journey decorated with coloured lights. The woman in black waiting to cross the road is the saddler John Donald's sister. Four years later, in 1912, she perhaps made a decision that had a bearing on her long life when she chose at the last minute not to sail on the *Titanic*.

The Electra Cinema in Cheadle High Street dressed overall for George V's silver jubilee in 1935. Two years later, in 1937, the bunting would come out again for George VI's coronation. Between Boots and the District Bank is a less familiar name still remembered with affection by some, the Shropshire Farm Produce shop.

A busy day in the High Street in the 1950s. Remember when it was fun to go into the village on your bike?

Wilmslow Road in 1908, when businesses included the Cheadle Fent Warehouse and Refreshment Rooms.

A similar scene in the early years of this century, showing both a tram and a horse-drawn bus parked outside the White Hart.

Wilmslow Road in the 1920s, with the wall of the then Rectory just off-picture on the left.

The scene in around 1950, on a less than bustling day.

The timeless grouping of the White Hart and St Mary's Church, upstaged for once by the Ovaltine girl in the early post-war years.

The White Hart en fête, possibly for the coronation of 1911. The large poster to the left, on the footpath in front of the hotel, appears to show pictures of elephants in various fanciful poses.

Chilly but charming. A lovely view of the White Hart and church in snow.

THE·OLD·TOLL·BAR··CHEADLE

Cheadle's old toll bar, at the entrance to Gatley Road beside the White Hart. It is clearly the end of an era, for an advertisement on the building announces the sale of the redundant toll houses, and doubtless the sedate looking gentlemen are playing some lofty role in all this. Happily, as is so often the case, some little boys have found their way on to the picture to lighten the proceedings.

A faded memento of a time now beyond living memory. The Gatley Road toll gate in a village so very different from the one we know today.

GEO. BUCKLEY,

Family Draper and Hosier,

HIGH STREET. CHEADLE.

All Prices framed on the principle of Small Profits & Quick Returns.

ALBERT WARBURTON, George Street, Cheadle,

Has on hand and is prepared to offer at Reasonable Prices the following list:

Round Boilers, Grate Fronts with or without Fall Bars, Saddles, False Sides and Bottoms, Coal Savers, Oven Shelves, Dampers, and Frame Sash Weights. Strong Coal Shovels, Spades, Forks, Fire Bricks, Backs. Gun Stocks always on hand. Hob Bars, Garden Grids, Road Grids, Stench Traps, Eave Spouting, Down Spouting, Heads and Shoes, Elbows and S. Bends, Bolts, Nuts, Coach Screws, Wrought & Cut Nails.

Horses shod with Eckford & Harkman's Patent Pad and the Charlie-Shoe.
LAWN MOWERS AND ALL GARDEN IMPLEMENTS GROUND AND SET.
Agent for Chapman's Horse, Sheep & Cattle Oils.   N.B.—Kitchen Ranges taken down & fitted up.

Church magazine advertisements from 1896. Albert Warburton, a member of a well-known local trading family, seems a busy man. . . .

A watercolour of Cheadle Rectory in the late eighteenth century, a classical façade disguising a far earlier building. The lady in the doorway is a daughter of the Revd Thomas Cripps, rector from 1775 to 1794. The Rectory was demolished in 1939, and the post office now stands in part of its grounds.

The rear of the Rectory in Edwardian times – clad in creeper and with standard roses setting off its restful looking garden.

Cheadle Rectory, in its nineteenth-century black-and-white finery, in the early years of this century.

Old Rectory Gardens and the early post-war Cheadle post office, strikingly modern in this picture but now a building showing distinct signs of wear.

The National School in Wilmslow Road, built in 1837, immediately before and during its demolition in 1969. The Somerfield supermarket now stands on the site, but the church still has use of the Upper Room meeting-place above the store.

HAPPIEST DAYS OF THEIR LIVES

National School children, Grade Six, early twentieth century.

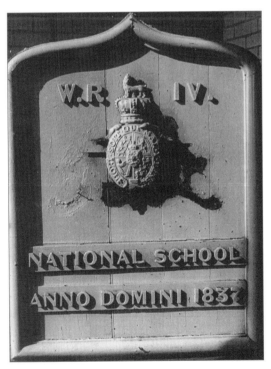

The National School plaque, placed on the building for its opening in 1837 but destroyed at the time of its demolition in 1969.

National School pupils, *c.* 1911–12.

The National School at around the beginning of the First World War. The teacher back left is thought to be Mrs Fowler, famous for her stinging back-handers. Back right is headmaster Mr Dives.

The National School at around the end of the First World War, with Mr Dives still the headmaster.

1st Cheadle Guides and Scouts, who formed a guard of honour at their captain's wedding, September 1932.

Brownies' grocery stall at All Saints' Church fête, Cheadle Hulme, November 1960. Early Granada TV personality Brian Trueman was the star guest.

9th and 11th Cheadle Hulme Guides and Brownies' concert, Cheadle Hulme Parish Hall, 1966.

Brownies' concert with a 'Children of All Nations' theme at Cheadle Hulme Parish Hall, 1968.

Some of the 1,300 Stockport area Guides reviewed by the county commissioner at Abney Hall in June 1928.

Presentation of Queen's Guide and other awards to eight Rangers, All Hallows, Cheadle, 1968.

St Mary's Church Girls' Brigade camp at Rhyl, *c.* 1920.

The beginning of a 1930s St Mary's Sunday School outing, when neatness and tidiness still prevailed.

What looks like a truckload of trouble, St Mary's Sunday School, 1930s.

Wheelbarrow races at a St Mary's Church Sunday School outing, possibly at Alderley Edge, 1930s.

A sunny day for the St Mary's Sunday School outing, June 1932.

Attentive St Mary's Sunday School pupils on their outing in June 1932, with their superintendent Ifor Illingworth Jones.

AROUND AND ABOUT

Barnes Convalescent Hospital was built for £26,000 in the 1870s. It was linked with Manchester Royal Infirmary. Another postcard view shows sheep grazing in the foreground meadow.

Barnes Hospital in around 1906. The group in the foreground consists of an elderly man and three boys, one of them on crutches. The message on the postcard from which this picture is taken, written by Alice to Miss Marsland in Stalybridge, reads: 'I do not like here. The place is very nice but I don't like the people. I went in the village on Monday. It was very nice and I bought a few postcards.'

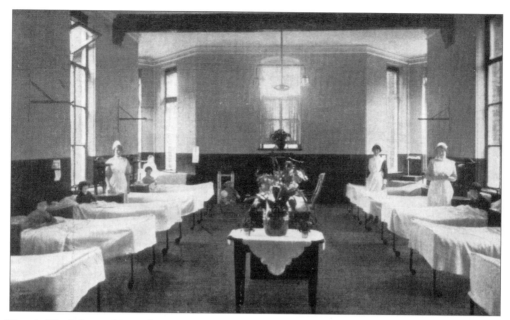

Victoria Ward, Barnes Hospital, 1935. This children's ward has its plus points – it is clean, light and airy, it is well staffed with three nurses, flowers are in evidence and at the back on the left there even seems to be a teddy bear sitting holding a ball. Minus points? Doesn't it all look rather sparse and spartan?

The Winter Gardens at Barnes Hospital, with well-starched nurses, and patients ranging from the elderly to little children. What a splendid conservatory this is; you can almost smell the heavy plant scents mingling with the disinfectant.

The lodge of the Manchester Warehousemen and Clerks' Orphan Schools, Cheadle Hulme, in Edwardian times.

Now Cheadle Hulme School, the Warehousemen and Clerks' Schools were built in 1869 at a cost of £15,000. The building is seen here in around 1920.

Another view of the Cheadle Hulme Schools.

The main entrance, Cheadle Royal. This psychiatric hospital still exists, though much of its surrounding land has been given over to a business park.

Grange Avenue on the Grange Estate, Cheadle Hulme, in 1938, its trees little more than saplings.

The now long demolished Hill Top Farm, Cheadle Hulme, in Edwardian times. Its brickwork appears neat enough, but the roofs look a packet of trouble.

Station Road, Cheadle Hulme, in the 1930s. Much has changed around here since then, and there is now a service station on the right.

A view of Church Road, Cheadle Hulme, taken from the corner of Ack Lane, *c.* 1905. On the left is All Saints' Vicarage; on the right, behind J.H. Bennett's grocer's van, the Church Inn.

W.F. Lees' hardware shop is to the right of this view of Ravenoak Road, Cheadle Hulme, in 1905.

Another of those long, empty Edwardian streets: Queen's Road, Cheadle Hulme.

Mellor Street, looking towards Cheadle Hulme station, in Edwardian times.

Hulme Hall Road, Cheadle Hulme, *c.* 1910, with the Old Cottage on the left.

The Old Cottage, Hulme Hall Road, Cheadle Hulme, now divided into two homes.

Hulme Hall, Cheadle Hulme, *c*. 1903. Dating in part from the sixteenth century, the hall was once a manor house owned by the Vernon family.

Hilltop Avenue, Cheadle Hulme, seen through a filter that makes it look like something out of Hollywood. Well, nearly. . . .

The front entrance of Bruntwood Hall, early 1950s. Once owned by the Porritt family and later by Cheadle and Gatley Urban District Council as its town hall, it is now used as offices.

The junction of Edgeley Road and Stockport Road, Cheadle Heath, where the Farmer's Arms still stands, with a little help from a Hungry Horse. The shops are, from left to right, Bradley's grocers, Wilks' hardware, Turner's newsagents and another food store, Parkinson's.

The Red Lion, Stockport Road, then a Bell's Ales house: This could well be a Sunday, for the children are in their best and the coachmen are in full livery.

The weir on the Micker Brook at Cheadle, *c.* 1920. This scene has scarcely changed in the years between – but post-war housing now hems the brook in to the right, and few modern mothers would encourage their little girls to play ring o' roses in the water. The Red Rocks were another popular spot for paddling in the brook in the inter-war years.

Old stone, cobbles, winter trees, bicycles: Schools Hill, Cheadle, *c.* 1905.

Outwood Road and Finney Lane, Heald Green, late 1950s. This is a scene of almost pre-war calm, with cyclists having the road all but to themselves.

Old brick, half timbering, mature trees and hedges: Stone Pale Road, Gatley, 1930s.

You could fire a gun. . . . The corner of Park Road, Gatley.

A bike ride and time to gossip over the gate: Pendlebury Road, Gatley.

A lonely spot: Four Lane Ends, Gatley, 1937.

Styal Road, Gatley, in 1926 – with a little fingerpost pointing to a remote hamlet called Ringway.

End of the line: the tram terminus at the Horse and Farrier at Gatley in the mid-1920s, beside the recently erected war memorial.

CHURCH LIFE

St Mary's Church, Cheadle, as portrayed in J.P. Earwaker's two excellent East Cheshire volumes of 1877.

A nineteenth-century print of St Mary's Church, showing its generations-old grouping with the White Hart hotel next door.

St Mary's Church , *c.* 1920.

An Edwardian walking day in the sun for Cheadle Parish Church girls.

Every aspect of parish church life was reflected in the walks of witness. Here we see the Girls' Brigade and the Mothers' Union.

The ringers of the bells of St Mary's in 1886. If they were off on a trip in that cart, it is to be hoped that it was not too far. An elderly but lively looking bunch, some of them must have been around at the time of the Napoleonic Wars. If we could travel back in time, what a lot we would wish to ask them about life in nineteenth-century England in general and Cheadle in particular. But how difficult would communication be, for their life seems a world away from ours.

A rather more sedate and young looking group of bellringers, 1902, though one or two old faces remain. In this part of Cheshire the last decade of the nineteenth century saw great suburbanization and strides, for better or worse, towards 'modern' life.

A picture from the Parish Church archives described as 'The Young Men of 1890', presumably a Bible class group. Two members of the Alcock family, John and George, are among them.

St Mary's choirboys in 1883, with their then young choirmaster Arthur Seddon to the rear. In the 1930s his sister Annie left a legacy to be invested to pay for an organist, a bequest that lives on to today.

St Mary's Parish Hall, the Sykes Memorial Hall in Ashfield Road, shortly before it was demolished to make way for an office development in the 1970s.

The north side of St Mary's churchyard, *c.* 1970. At the centre of the aisle wall, cleaner stone still surrounds the window that replaced the north door in Victorian times while to the right, still gleaming, is the functional but very necessary toilet block of the late 1960s.

In characteristic pose, the late Alan Stain chronicles yet another gravestone in Cheadle churchyard. Thanks to his efforts, the church has an exhaustive record of the people buried in its grounds, and the inscriptions by which they are remembered.

The Revd John Cumming Macdona was Rector of the Parish Church from 1874 until 1883, when he resigned to become an MP and made his post vacant for his brother, Frederick Augustus (see p. 96). The west window was donated by J.C. Macdona's son, and several of the characters in the window have been depicted as likenesses of members of the Macdona family. The father, seen here, is portrayed as Timothy's father, the Greek.

The Revd William Brown Pollock was Rector from 1917 until 1936, and died in 1949. He was St Mary's second rector of the twentieth century, and only four have succeeded him.

Canon William James Wilkinson, Rector from 1936 until his death in 1953, seen with his wife and other younger clergymen. Len Ashton, to the rear on the right, went on to become a senior chaplain for the RAF.

The Revd John Gordon Kitchener Harman, Rector from 1954 until 1960, when he went on to become Rector of Edgware. He retired in 1979.

The eleventh-century preaching cross found in Cheadle in around 1874. It is now displayed in the Parish Church's Savage Chapel and is widely used as a symbol locally, not least as the badge of Cheadle Primary School.

Canon James Ayre in characteristic pose in the old National Schoolroom, instructing, entertaining and delighting Sunday School pupils after a concert. He was Rector from 1961 until his retirement in 1988. He died in 1994.

The induction of the present Rector of Cheadle, the Revd Donald Spargo Allister, in April 1989. With him are the then Bishop of Chester, the Rt Revd Michael Baughn, and the Venerable John Gaisford, then Archdeacon of Macclesfield and now Bishop of Beverley. They are unveiling the revised roll of rectors, with the Revd Mr Allister's name added to it.

The late 1960s, and the building of All Hallows' Anglican church. It was opened in 1970 as a daughter to Cheadle Parish Church, but became a separate parish in 1982.

1837.

Receipts of the Bazaar held May 9th 10th 11th

	£	s	d
Mrs Leigh —	140	0	0
Mrs Lane —	33	18	0
Mrs Lupton —	41	12	6
Miss Thomson	52	15	6
Miss Harding —	110	..	..
Mr G Reid & Miss Baxter	123	13	0
Refreshment	12	1	8
Received at the Doors	69	17	0
£	583	17	8
Deduct Expences £	39	..	..
Bazaar Receipts £	544	17	8
Subscriptions —	325	11	5
Sermons —	28	..	..
Interest from Bank	2	8	3
Slates & Bricks sold	2	1	6
National Society's Grant	90	..	..
Treasury Grant —	90	..	..
£	1082	19	10
Deduct expences of School £	650	5	5
	432	13	5
For the Endowment of Handford Chapel	400	..	..
School at Handford	20	..	..
Repairs of Heath School	13	13	5

1837.

Expences in building the National Sunday School

	£	s	d
Mr Bancroft for the site	90	10	0
Mr Tinston Solicitor	6	2	0
... for Bricks —	22	13	6
Carting do	4	8	0
Chandley Bricksetter	43	14	0
Darbyshire Stone mason	93	12	0
Barlow for Bricks —	24	9	8
Ludlow Stock Bricks	9	11	6
Bowden Slates —	26	8	0
Green for lime	6	9	0
Savage carting —	7	10	3
Haughton & Woodall —	2	12	9
Chapman & Woodcock —	1	18	6
Faulkner & Smethurst	2	18	0
Aycock Plumber & Glazier	48	10	0
Harrop Painter —	41	0	0
Jones Joiner —	160	0	0
Benches, ...	19	6	0
Iron rails —	17	0	0
grates —	4	13	0
Warburton Blacksmith	7	0	0
gravel & labor —	1	18	3
Savage carting —	1	6	0
Chandley	6	14	6
£	650	5	5

Expenses for building the National Sunday School in 1837 totalled £650 5s 5d, of which a grand bazaar over three days in May raised £544 17s 8d. This is the church record of those times, and a happy tale it tells. With grants and subscriptions there was more than £1,000 in the kitty, and £400 was endowed to build St Chad's Chapel at Handforth.

TRANSPORTS OF DELIGHT

Various dignitaries aboard the stagecoach that ran from the White Hart to the Spread Eagle in Manchester in the summers of 1876 to '79. The journey took forty-five minutes, arriving in Manchester at 9.15 a.m. and leaving the city at 5 p.m. The coachman is Dick Wood and the apparently small figure at the front next to him is the Revd J.C. Macdona.

The tram at the Cheadle Green halt, beside the fountain, the poplars giving the view an almost Continental air.

Maintaining the railway. Included in the group of workmen are Mr Lamb, William Wilson and Mr Cooper.

Cheadle station, *c.* 1870, with the crew of a Crewe goods type 2–4–0 tank engine.

Cheadle station, *c.* 1895.

Cheadle station less than a-bustle in 1905.

A Sentinel railcar on the Stockport to Warrington line in the 1930s.

Gatley station under construction, *c.* 1908. A timber-framed building, it looks here more like a Wild West halt than leafy Cheshire.

An evocative view of Gatley station during its early years.

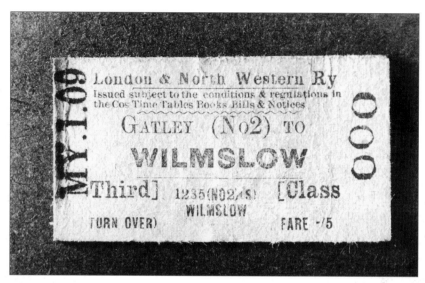

Fivepence was once the fare from Gatley to Wilmslow, if, like most people, you were happy to settle for third class. This ticket was issued on Gatley station's opening day.

The first passenger train to arrive at Gatley station is eagerly awaited, 1 May 1909.

The first train in Gatley station, 1 May 1909.

MEET THE FOLKS

Silk stockings and some convincing looking antique furniture. The Players' production of *The Best People* at Cheadle Hulme Village Hall, February 1935.

J.M. Barrie's *The Professor's Love Story* was the Cheadle Hulme Players' production of February 1937. Among well-remembered figures in the picture are Arnold Clough, Robert Goodwin and Zena Davy.

A production of *Caesar's Friend*, October 1938, put on in Cheadle Hulme Parish Hall by the Vicar of Cheadle Hulme, the Revd W.L. Beckles Goodwin, who played Pilate. The producer was Robert Goodwin, a prominent name in local amateur dramatic circles.

At Cheadle Hulme Parish Hall, the Players' *Dear Octopus* in February 1948. Though fêted in the West End and on Broadway, the writer of the play, Dodie Smith, was a Manchester girl.

The Players' *Worm's Eye View*, November 1952.

Black faces and big eyes: Jean Thomson and Mollie Green in *South Sea Bubble*, 1960. The Cheadle Hulme Players moved into their own purpose-built playhouse in 1955.

Cheadle Parish Church 'effort', 1932. With due respect, how much effort constituted an 'effort'?

Cheadle Hulme Players' Christmas Fair, 1960, and plenty of cheerful faces. It would be pleasant to say that the bric-a-brac contains gems now worth thousands – but it doesn't.

Parish Church children's summer holiday club, with a Cutty Sark theme, early 1970s.

Parish traders' outing, 1912. Alcocks, Warburtons, Carrs and Marshes are all here – not to mention Marjorie Macdona, an actress member of the long-serving family of rectors.

A church group, late Victorian times, very possibly a wedding since the women's hats are decorated with flowers and the men wear buttonholes to brighten their dark clothing.

Mr Howard, Miss Gill and Mrs Mottershead are in this group around a pony-drawn milk cart. Presumably they are declaring their political allegiance, since they are outside the Liberal Association offices and news room.

Scenes at a high day, both of them most probably the coronation of 1911. Above, local volunteers are seen with the Revd F.A. Macdona, while below, a great assembly celebrates the crowning of George V.

The celebrated Victorian medical practitioner Dr Ockleston. Fletcher Moss recorded several stories about him in his book of 1894, though none seems very funny now. Influential men in small communities were often very much creatures of their time and place. This is the man commemorated by the fountain that stood for decades at the head of the High Street near Cheadle Green.

J. ALCOCK,
THE BAZAAR, CHEADLE,
DEALER IN
Drapery, Hosiery, and Fancy Goods.

A LIBERAL BONUS TO DORCAS AND CLOTHING CLUBS

GENERAL UNDERTAKER.

FOR SUMMER'S SUN AND WINTER'S WIND.

PRITCHARD'S
Glycerine and Cucumber:
RENDERS THE SKIN SOFT, SUPPLE. AND SMOOTH

WHITE COUGH MIXTURE | BRONCHITIS MIXTURE
FOR CHILDREN. | FOR ADULTS.

Prepared by J. PRITCHARD, Chemist, CHEADLE, Manchester,
Proprietor of the celebrated Teething and Fever Powders.

CHEADLE FAMILY BOOT DEPOT,
85 & 87, HIGH STREET.

Ladies', Gentlemen's, and Children's Boots, Shoes and Slippers in all kinds and styles, suitable for all seasons.

—— REPAIRS AND MEASURES ON THE PREMISES. ——

E. BLACKER.
CLOSED ON WEDNESDAYS AT ONE P.M.

Church magazine advertisements of 1896. The Alcock family name is still attached to separate drapery and undertaking businesses, but here it seems odd to see funerals and fancy goods advertised side by side.

THIS SPORTING LIFE

A Cheadle Heath Cricket Club First XI of the early post-war years.

Cheadle Hulme Cricket Club enjoyed a memorable season in 1978, winning both the Cheshire County League and the county knock-out trophy as well as a number of lesser awards. The club even made its mark on a wider field by reaching the quarter-finals of the John Haig national competition. Back row, left to right: N.T. O'Brien, R.E.S. Green, M. Thomas, D.A. Sparks, D.K. Beckett, R.I. Brown, S. Thompson, D.H. Bourne (umpire). Front row: W. Miller, M. Woods, E.J. Pimlott (captain), J.S. Howarth, R.R. Locke, J.K. Leach. Another regular player that season was A. Mosedale.

Cheadle St Mary's footballers at the end of a successful 1925/6 season.

Colin Barrett was a Cheadle Hulme Nomads product who went on to enjoy success with Manchester United and Nottingham Forest in the 1970s. Another distinguished ex-Nomad was Harry Catterick, who served Everton as both a player and manager.

Back in the 1920s there was always a chance that the *Stockport Advertiser*'s cartoonist George Butterworth would look in on your match and immortalize you in a way that would have you carrying his handiwork in your wallet or purse for the rest of your life. Here he is, in the typically heavy-handed style of the day, at a hockey match between two of the top five teams in the Stockport league of 1922/3, Christy's AC and Primrose of Cheadle Hulme.

The two Cheadle Heath Junior Sports Club teams in the Stockport and District Hockey League in 1922/3. The first team (above), with their dog mascot on the left, were first division champions, while the second team (below) were runners-up in division two. Their doll mascot is held by the girl second from the left on the back row.

The pavilion at Gorsey Bank Park, Cheadle, in the early 1960s.

Cheadle Heath Nomads, 1923/4, with committee members.

A Cheadle Heath Nomads side of the 1930s, in white rather than their now familiar claret and blue.

A fine season for Cheadle Heath Nomads, 1950/1. Many of the lads were out of the Forces and happily settled back in Civvy Street, and to be a member of a successful soccer team was the icing on the cake.

Time to celebrate: a cup-laden Cheadle Heath Nomads group, *c.* 1960.

June 1986, and a last glimpse, above, of Cheadle Heath Sports Club's old clubhouse in a lucrative deal that saw a plot of land sold for house building. Another welcome spin-off was the opening of a new clubhouse, seen celebrated by members and committee men, below.

Time to end this book – in Cheadle Time, of course. Most of us know by now that the messages on the three clock faces, introduced in 1988, read FORGET NOT GOD on the porch side, TRUST THE LORD on the White Hart side, and TIME IS FLYING on the car park side. But that does not make these odd combinations of letters any less distracting, turning the simple process of telling the time into a brain-teaser. For some reason the Y in FLYING throws many onlookers – but what a quirky legacy for the go-getting 1980s to leave future generations of Cheadle residents.

ACKNOWLEDGEMENTS

Thanks for the loan of pictures, background information and other help are due to:

the Revd Donald Allister • Margaret Brookes • Cheadle Heath Sports Club
Cheadle Hulme Cricket Club • Muriel Cunningham • Dr George Chivers • David Fisher
Basil Jeuda • Eileen Knight • Rod Macaulay • Players Dramatic Society • Dora Steele
Roy Welsh • Ena Wint

BRITAIN IN OLD PHOTOGRAPHS

To order any of these titles please telephone our distributor, Littlehampton Book Services on 01903 721596
For a catalogue of these and our other titles please ring Regina Schinner on 01453 731114